The Siege

The Siege

UNDER ATTACK IN RENAISSANCE EUROPE

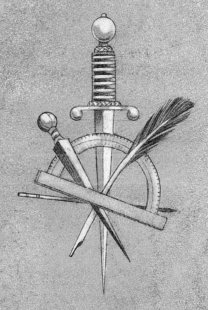

by Stephen Shapiro

art by John Mantha

annick press

toronto + new york + vancouver

Annick Press Ltd.

We acknowledge the support of the Canada Council for the Arts, the Ontario Arts Council, and the Government of Canada through the Book Publishing Industry Development Program (BPIDP) for our publishing activities.

Cataloging in Publication

Shapiro, Stephen, date-
      The siege : under attack in Renaissance Europe / by Stephen Shapiro ; art by John Mantha.

Includes index.
ISBN-13: 978-1-55451-108-2 (bound)
ISBN-10: 1-55451-108-9 (bound)
ISBN-13: 978-1-55451-107-5 (pbk.)
ISBN-10: 1-55451-107-0 (pbk.)

1. Siege warfare—Europe—History—16th century—Juvenile literature.
2. Sieges—Netherlands—History—Juvenile literature. I. Mantha, John II. Title.

UG444.S46 2007   j355.4'409409031   C2007-900707-4

The text was typeset in Caslon LT Std Antique and New Baskerville.

Distributed in Canada by: Published in the U.S.A. by Annick Press (U.S.) Ltd.
Firefly Books Ltd.   Distributed in the U.S.A. by:
66 Leek Crescent   Firefly Books (U.S.) Inc.
Richmond Hill, ON   P.O. Box 1338
L4B 1H1   Ellicott Station
                           Buffalo, NY 14205

Printed and bound in China

Visit us at: www.annickpress.com

To Anne
 —S.S.

To my wife, Leanne
 —J.M.

Map of the Netherlands 1585

N

NORTH SEA

The star marks the place where the fictitious town of Berkdorp is located.

Haarlem

Amsterdam

Naarden

Zutphen

HOLLAND

★

Maas River

Antwerp

Mechlen

Liège

Namur

Contents

The Town of Berkdorp

Marsh

Marsh

Crownwork

Moat

The Church

The Town Hall

Ravelin

Hornwork

The road from Antwerp

The road to Holland

Maas River

In 1585 the Netherlands were in revolt against the Spanish Empire, and Spanish armies were besieging many Dutch towns. The story you are about to read is based on many of those sieges. While some of the people and places in this book are real, the town of Berkdorp, its inhabitants, and the Spanish army that besieges it are not. Instead, they are modeled on real people and places of the time. All details are as historically accurate as possible, but are not based on any one event.

1492: Columbus reaches the Americas.

1506: Leonardo da Vinci paints the MONA LISA.

1517: Martin Luther begins the Reformation.

1521: Spanish conquistadors defeat the Aztec Empire in Mexico.

1534: Jacques Cartier reaches Canada.

1562: Wars of Religion begin in France.

1566: The Dutch revolt begins.

1585: OUR STORY

1588: The Spanish Armada defeated by the English navy.

1598: Edict of Nantes ends the French Wars of Religion.

1607: First English settlement in America, at Jamestown.

1610: Galileo uses the telescope to discover the moons of Jupiter.

1648: Peace of Westphalia ends the Dutch revolt.

    The Dutch Republic is born.

The Message

The wind was wild. It whipped at the horse and rider as they sped along the road. Branches overhead scratched at the man's head, ripping his hat. Exhausted from his long journey, the messenger tightened his coat around himself, fighting off the chill. His eyes searched for any signs of danger. Years of war had driven ex-soldiers to become brigands. They hid in the woods and robbed unwary travelers. He had been lucky to avoid them so far.

After a few more minutes of hard riding, the messenger broke out of the forest. Neatly tilled fields streaked by on either side. Peasants hard at work in the fields gave him startled glances as he raced by. Ahead he saw the walls of the town rising up. The gates were open, with only a few soldiers standing idly around. No doubt more of them were in the guardhouse, playing dice.

A flurry of activity began when the rider galloped into view, with soldiers grabbing their weapons and adjusting their armor. The rider reigned in his horse and halted in front of them. The guards were there to watch everyone who came into or left the town. Strangers had to give the guards their name and the name of the inn they were lodging at.

Luckily, the rider was not a stranger. He was a servant of the States-General, the leaders of the Dutch revolt, and the guards recognized him. Once he passed through the gates, he was only a few minutes from Berkdorp's town hall. There, he could finally deliver his message from the headquarters of the rebel Dutch army.

Arriving at the hall, the rider found only a few clerks going over the tax rolls. They scurried off to find the members of the town council – the prosperous merchants and master craftsmen who governed the town. Once they were assembled, the messenger could deliver his warning: a Spanish army approached!

| January | February | March | April | May | June | July | August | September | October | November | December |

Sentries on the town
wall stand guard.

11

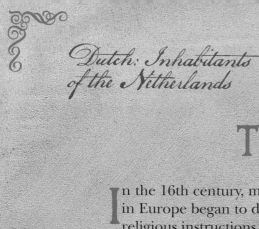

The Dutch Revolt

In the 16th century, many Christians in Europe began to disagree with the religious instructions of the Catholic Church. They started to follow church leaders such as Martin Luther or John Calvin, who were called Protestants. The southern part of the Netherlands (now called Belgium) was still mostly Catholic. But the north (still known as the Netherlands today) was one of the places where Protestantism was the strongest.

Rich and prosperous, the Netherlands were packed with towns and cities. In fact, its population of three million made the region the most populated in Europe. For hundreds of years the towns of the Netherlands had also had special rights – to choose their own leaders, build their own walls, to levy taxes and tolls, even to mint coins.

The Netherlands were part of the Spanish Empire, the most powerful in Europe. The king of Spain, Philip II, was a devoted Catholic. He had even told the Pope he would rather lose his lands and die than have to rule over Protestants. So when more and more Dutch started becoming Protestants, Philip sent his armies to the Netherlands to enforce Catholicism and Spanish rule. In the south, where most of the people were still Catholic, they had no trouble doing this. But in the north, the Protestant Dutch, led by William the Silent, Prince of Orange, raised an army and fought back. Even the Catholics in the north joined the Protestants, afraid that Philip would take away their towns' rights.

Dutch rebels called Sea Beggars captured Spanish ships, while the Beggars of the Woods ambushed Spanish patrols. Eventually Philip had to send his greatest general, the Prince of Parma, to the Netherlands to fight the rebels. In late 1584, Parma was besieging the port of Antwerp and planning his next move. Once Antwerp fell, Parma wanted to march north and invade Holland – the rebel heartland. To reach Holland his men would have to cross the Maas River, but all the bridges were guarded by rebel towns. Parma wrote to King Philip, asking for more men to capture one of the towns and open up a route into Holland. If they failed, Parma's invasion would be fatally delayed.

The Pope is the head of the Roman Catholic Church.

■ Spanish Empire

An Army on the Road

The Spanish army – 15,000 soldiers and 12,000 civilian **camp followers** – lumbered northwards. Its columns stretched for miles as they marched towards the rebel town. The troops had come from all over the Spanish Empire, assembling in northern Italy. They were taking the route to the Netherlands that kings and generals called the Spanish Road.

It was not an easy trip. The men would march from Milan to the Spanish base at Namur, 1,100 grueling kilometers (700 miles). Local guides were essential. They led the troops along winding roads and through deep forests. Commanders also relied on primitive route maps that showed bridges, forests, alternate paths, and nearby towns.

The soldiers rarely had the chance to sleep in real beds. If they were **billeted** in local homes, the men often ran wild. They stole silverware and animals and sometimes burned down the entire village. Towns locked their gates as the army passed by. It was easier for everyone, except the soldiers themselves, if they slept in the countryside – under hedges or in primitive huts they built called *barracas*. Only in the harsh weather of

the mountains did officers make sure the soldiers had solid shelters.

The most difficult task during the trip was making sure the army was properly fed. An army of 27,000 people was like a walking city – and needed as much food as one that stood still. An army on the move could always let its soldiers loose to get what they needed from the locals – often without paying. On the Spanish Road, however, the Spanish commanders knew that such behavior would be a terrible mistake. They needed the peasants on their side. Food was provided in a more orderly fashion: the *étapes* system.

Planning for the *étapes* began long before the army set out from Italy. Merchants were hired to bring food to where the soldiers would be staying each night. This gave the merchants time to buy food and transport it to the Spanish Road. They handed the provisions out to the troops and were paid directly by the army paymaster. The soldiers themselves never had to worry about their next meal – it was already taken care of.

The prices were also set well in advance. If food was plentiful, the merchant could buy it cheaply and sell it to the army for a hefty profit. If food was scarce and prices high, the merchant still had to honor the contract, even if it meant he lost money selling to the army. No one wanted to break a contract with the Spanish king – the most powerful in Europe.

Being organized meant that the army would make good time, reaching the gates of Namur after 48 days on the road. Each day's march brought the army closer to its target, the town of Berkdorp. Its progress was beyond concealment, and news of its destination spread.

| January | February | March | April | May | June | July | August | September | October | November | December |

The Netherlands

France

Spain

Italy

Billeted: Sent to live in people's homes.

Camp follower: Anyone who lives with but isn't in the army — women, children, merchants, etc.

The Siege Begins

Stiff from his long journey, the rider delivered his timely message. Berkdorp still had a few days before the Spanish forces arrived – days that might make the difference between victory and defeat.

The messenger's warning meant that Berkdorp would not fall to a surprise assault. There were many ways communities had been taken by surprise. Enemy soldiers had sneaked in through sewers, or had been hidden under cargo in a boat entering the town. Then, at the right moment, the invaders swarmed out of hiding and captured the town. A less secretive but very effective method was to wedge a wagon between the doors of the town gate, stopping it from closing, then rush troops in. But none of these schemes would work if the guards knew some sort of attack was coming.

The townspeople made good use of their time. They quickly began to demolish the buildings nearest Berkdorp, outside the walls. It was against the law to build houses immediately outside the walls, because they would block sentries on the town wall from seeing approaching enemies. Despite this rule, small suburbs had grown up beyond the protected area once the space inside the walls had all been used. These homes and workshops were now razed to the ground, leaving nowhere for the Spanish to hide as they approached the fortress. The people who lived in the suburbs fled into the town.

Berkdorp also began to stockpile food. The siege would make it almost impossible to obtain more food, so every bushel of grain counted. In extreme cases, a town under siege might even expel women and children as "useless mouths" they could not afford to feed. The Dutch were not so harsh.

Soon the first Spanish **cavalry** appeared on the horizon, driving the last of the townspeople behind the safety of the town walls. Three days later, the main Spanish army arrived. With it came the Spaniards' *siege train* – the heavy guns that would batter down the walls of Berkdorp. The guns were so heavy that, while the rest of the army traveled on land, they had to come by river barge.

The first task of the **besiegers** was to construct two sets of their own fortifications. The *lines of countervallation* faced inwards and stopped the defenders from breaking out. The *lines of circumvallation* faced outwards, preventing any reinforcements from reaching the town. They would also protect the Spanish troops if the main Dutch army arrived to attack them. Both sets of lines consisted of earthworks, dirt walls, and little forts called *redoubts*.

Besiegers: The army that lays siege to a town or fortress.

Cavalry: Soldiers who fight from horseback.

| January | February | March | April | May | June | July | August | September | October | November | December |

Berkdorp

Boats tied together prevent the
Dutch sailing downriver.

Lines of circumvallation

Lines of countervallation

Spanish camp

The Soldier's Life

The soldiers who served the Spanish king in the Netherlands – known as the Army of Flanders – were a varied and ragged bunch. Most had joined the army in their twenties. Some had done it for the sense of adventure, others to escape a stinking jail cell. Most had found themselves out of work and signed up to avoid starvation.

In camp the men spent most of their wages on meat and wine, which they bought from traders, called *sutlers*, who trailed after the army. They had to buy bread from the army – a pound and a half of mixed rye and wheat each day. The bread was often disgusting, mixed with broken biscuits, chunks of plaster, or raw grains. This kept the costs down for the baker, but could make the soldiers sick.

The soldiers wore striking clothes – colorful and fancy, but reduced to tatters by the rigors of the campaign. In Spanish lands the laws forbade peasants from wearing such finery in order to prevent confusion between nobles, towns-people, and servants. But when fighting in the Netherlands, the generals believed it was "the finery, the plumes, and the bright colors" that gave "spirit and strength to a soldier," making him a better fighter. No army in Europe at that time required its men to wear uniforms. Spanish soldiers, for example, had to wear a red sash or scarf to identify them in battle.

The men were recruited from all over Europe, and most of the soldiers envied the real Spaniards in the army. Considered the best troops, they were paid much more than the men from other nations. The Italians got nearly as much, while the local Dutch were paid the least. This was because the Spanish crown believed that troops fought best away from home: "There is no surer strength than that of foreign soldiers." The lure of higher wages encouraged some to conceal their nationality: a quarter of the "Spanish" light cavalry in the Army of Flanders were actually Walloons (men from the southern-most part of the Netherlands).

Even the real Spaniards weren't paid particularly well. A soldier's daily wage was less than that of a farm laborer. Then he had to pay the army for bread and the other goods it provided. A musketeer might even be charged for the gunpowder he used to fire his weapon!

The best-paid soldiers were the gentle-men rankers, called *particulares*. They were young nobles, often relatives of the captain of the company they served in. Gentlemen rankers were supposed to inspire the other soldiers to do their best. Most were poor nobles who saw employment in the army, even as a simple soldier, as a respectable source of income. Others, such as the dukes of Osuna and Pastrana, were rich youths without an officer's commission who hoped to be noticed by a commander and rise to a more important position in the army.

19

Breaking Ground

General
Don Luis
de Guevara

Once the lines of circumvallation and counter-vallation were safely under construction, the besiegers turned their attention to the town itself. Attacking Berkdorp from all sides would divide and weaken the attacker's forces. Instead, they would choose a single side of the fortress to receive a crushing attack.

Selecting the point of attack was important, so Don Luis de Guevara, the Spanish general, decided he would examine the town walls in person. Like many military men, Don Luis was the youngest son of one of the great Spanish nobles. He had started his military career when he was only 11, becoming the page to an old general. The boy's duties were to carry messages for his master on the battlefield and serve his meals at home. He had ridden, hunted, and fenced, training his body for war. After a few years as a page, he had been made a lieutenant. Over the years he had risen gradually through the ranks to his position as general. He had read a few books on war, but most of what he knew he had learned from personal experience.

Riding his horse around the Dutch walls, the general was an obvious target. Every Dutch musket and cannon blazed away at him, but he was just far enough away that he rode through the gun-fire unharmed. Don Luis also sent other officers forward – on foot – to make sketches of the defenses. They went in pairs, one watching the defender's guns as the other sketched. If the first noticed the guns about to fire, both men threw themselves to the ground – and hoped the shot would fly over their heads.

His personal observations confirmed what Don Luis de Guevara already knew: a direct assault was hopeless against this fortress. If he ordered an assault, his men would have to march unconcealed across the open ground surrounding the fort (called its **glacis**), then cross the fort's **moat** and scale its walls – all under constant bombardment from the fortress guns. He would be throwing his army away.

Trenches
The first trenches were dug by handpicked men working at night.

| January | February | March | April | May | June | July | August | September | October | November | December |

Moat: A water-filled ditch surrounding a fortification (also called a wet ditch).

Glacis: The cleared area surrounding a fortress that provides no cover for an attacker.

Parks
The Spanish placed excess siege equipment in parks.

Magazines
Magazines kept gunpowder away from people and equipment in case the powder exploded.

Grand Battery
The heaviest Spanish guns were set up together as the Grand Battery.

Don Luis called for his chief engineer and they made a plan. The Spanish would dig zigzag **trenches** towards the fortress, coming closer and closer until they reached the edge of the moat. The zigzags made it impossible for a single Dutch cannonball to bounce its way down the entire length of the trench, killing troops and wreaking havoc. Spanish cannons at the front of the trenches would blast a hole in the wall. Then the attackers' **infantry** could storm up out of the trenches and through the breach without ever having to cross the glacis in the open at all.

Taking advantage of any available shelter – the Dutch had missed a few buildings when they burned the suburbs – the Spanish army pitched its camp opposite the part of the wall chosen as the target of the attack. The artillery and siege equipment were lined up in open **parks**. Gunpowder was placed in **magazines**, surrounded by earthen walls that would contain the explosion if the stocks caught fire (by accident or enemy action). The heaviest guns were placed together in a **grand battery**, where – protected by earthworks – they would harass the gunners of the fortress.

All that remained was to begin the digging by "breaking ground." Guarded by specially selected troops, diggers began to excavate the first trenches. The defenders were sure to respond to any digging with a hefty cannonade, so the digging began secretly at night. With any luck, these first trenches would be ready by first light, without the enemy even knowing they existed. With the "opening of the trenches," the real siege began.

Infantry: Soldiers who fight on foot.

Mighty Walls

Twenty years earlier Berkdorp had torn down its tall, decaying medieval walls. In their place had been erected low, thick walls and squat **bastions**. The *trace italienne* had arrived.

The spread of cannons nearly a century earlier had allowed the armies of Europe to smash the defenses of their opponents. The *trace italienne* was a response to the cannon. Brilliant Italian engineers had seen that lower walls would make a smaller target for cannons, and thicker walls (made mostly of packed earth) would be harder to destroy. At first these earthen walls were used as a last resort – built quickly behind tall walls about to be destroyed – but eventually they became the main line of defense. By adding a ditch in front of the wall, the engineers made it as hard to scale as the earlier tall walls had been. Instead of round or square towers, they now used four-sided bastions, which left no spaces for the enemy to hide. Both walls and bastions were lined with cannons.

Many of these early Italian designers were also great Renaissance artists. Michelangelo Buonarroti, most famous as the painter of the Sistine Chapel and sculptor of the great *David*, was also a Florentine inspector of fortifications. He once said, "I don't know very much about painting and sculpture, but I have gained a great experience of fortifications." The great artist and inventor Leonardo da Vinci, painter of the *Mona Lisa*, was also a fortress designer for the city of Florence. Many other fortress planners were jewelers or goldsmiths. All of them produced fortress plans as well crafted as any of their works of art.

Taking the *trace italienne* from its home in Italy to the northern lands of Holland required modifications that became known as the "Old Netherlandish" style. Firstly, unlike the plains of Italy, the lowlands of the Netherlands were filled with rivers and lakes. Because of this, dry ditches were replaced in northern designs with water-filled wet ditches. Secondly, the rebellious Dutch had no time or money for long and expensive construction projects. Instead of using stone to shape the earthen walls, as the Italians did, the Dutch built their fortress walls solely of dirt. This was much cheaper, although it did make them easier to climb (an earthen wall sloped downwards at the front instead of standing vertical, like one with a stone face). To make climbing a little more difficult, the Dutch often stuck storm poles – horizontal spikes of wood – into the earth of the walls. These might trip up or stab careless attackers.

Tall, thin walls were hard to climb but easy for cannons to hit and destroy. The lower, thicker walls of the trace italienne were harder to hit and harder to destroy.

Bastions are low, four-sided towers designed with no blind spots. Unlike square or round towers, every spot on a bastion's face can be seen from the town's main wall. There is nowhere for an attacker to hide.

Advancing the Sap

The Spanish trenches slowly began to creep towards Berkdorp's walls. The army's chief engineer, Fabrizio Strozzi, had set the plan of attack. Strozzi was, like the greatest fortress designers of the age, Italian. Born in Milan, he had served first the Milanese, then the French, and now the Spanish. He was loyal to Spain as long as his pay arrived regularly. Now he took a fresh page of parchment to lay out the lines his trenches should follow.

European soldiers – and the Spanish were no exception – considered the digging of trenches dirty and beneath them. No matter how often generals tried to set an example by doing a little digging themselves, soldiers never considered it real soldiering. Extra pay could usually convince a soldier to work with a spade, but that was expensive. Instead, the army scoured the countryside looking for peasants who could be convinced to do the heavy digging. Peasants might run away before the siege was done, but they were cheaper than soldiers.

Working steadily, the men dug the zigzag trenches towards the walls. Each leg of the trench, called a *sap*, was usually 130 meters (142 yards) long and dug a meter (three feet) deep. Digging in the Netherlands was a little more difficult than in the rest of Europe. Underground water lay only a few feet beneath the surface. Normal trenches would be flooded, and so the Spanish besiegers dug shallower ones. The earth from the trench was dumped into *gabions* (wicker baskets open at the top and bottom), which were piled up to line the sides of the trench

and give some protection from gunfire.

As the trenches advanced, more men followed behind to widen and deepen them. Well-trained diggers, called *sappers*, could extend a trench by 6 meters (19.5 feet) in an hour, placing five or six gabions along its edges.

Being at the front of the sap was extremely dangerous. The **garrison** knew that killing the workers was the only way to stop the constant advance of the besiegers. The Dutch fired their cannons and muskets continuously at the advancing trenches. The sappers gained some protection by sheltering behind a *sap-roller* (a filled gabion on its side) or *mantlet* (a wooden shield on wheels), but it was never enough. Although each man's shift lasted only an hour, two-thirds of the sappers were killed while working.

The Spanish sappers were well paid for their risky work. They might receive up to 20 times the normal wages. The danger of their job made the sappers reckless. One engineer observed that they had "a tendency to get drunk while they are working at the head [front] of a sap. They throw every precaution to the winds and have themselves killed off like brute beasts."

Fabrizio Strozzi observed with pleasure that the sappers were making good progress. There was no shortage of volunteers this time, and there would be sappers at least until the money ran out. Unless the Dutch found some way to disrupt his carefully calculated schedule, the trenches would reach the moat within two months. The only question was, how would the Dutch respond?

Garrison: The men
stationed in a town
to defend it.

The Army of Flanders

With 60,000 men spread all across the Netherlands, structure was vital to the Army of Flanders. Organization gave the army its impressive fighting power, and the Spanish their reputation as excellent soldiers.

The basic **unit** of the army was the company. All the men in a company came from the same nation, so Germans fought alongside Germans and Spaniards alongside Spaniards. The company was the soldier's world. He lived, ate, and trained within it. Where the company was sent, he went.

The company's captain had almost unlimited powers over his men. He usually recruited them himself. He chose the company's sergeants and corporals. He could strike, flog, or humiliate men at will. He also controlled the company finances. When pay was late, as it usually was, the captain loaned money to his men so they could survive – putting them even further in his debt. Moving to a new company was difficult. The only way to transfer away from a hated sergeant or officer was at a **muster** of the entire army. These happened very rarely.

In theory, each company consisted of 200 to 250 men. Sickness, injuries, desertion, and battle casualties often brought that number down to 150 or fewer. Some months a company might lose one out of every 14 men to sickness or desertion – even when there was no battle.

As commander of his company, an enterprising captain could make money for himself in a number of ways. State funds for buying equipment might be spent on cheaper materials, with the captain pocketing the savings. Civilians or camp followers could be enrolled in the unit as "soldiers," appearing on payday to be counted but never actually serving in the field. The captain would pay these pretenders a small bribe and keep the rest of their pay. Because captaincies were so profitable, the captains of tiny companies fought to keep their units separate, instead of letting their troops be merged into full-sized units. Reformation – combining companies – became a punishment for officers caught misusing official funds.

Ten to twenty companies of the same nationality were organized into a larger formation – for Spanish men a *tercio*, for others a *regiment*. This was a large and clumsy formation, suited only for the biggest battles. For fighting in the Netherlands, the army was more often organized into smaller, more flexible units called *squadrons*. Unlike a *tercio* or regiment, a squadron mixed companies of Spanish, German, and other troops to produce a force tailored to whatever job was at hand.

The army that besieged Berkdorp was like many other forces in the Army of Flanders. Three regiments of Germans (5,500 men in total) and two of Catholic Dutchmen (3,500 men) made up the bulk of the force; 900 light cavalrymen scouted and guarded its flanks; and two squadrons (2,500 men each) mixed Germans, Italians, and Burgundians (from what is now part of eastern France) with a hard core of Spanish veterans.

Unit: Any group of soldiers who fight together.

Muster: An assembly of the troops for inspection.

Pitch: A sticky substance made from tar and turpentine.

The Defenders

Inside the town, tensions were rising. The citizens had never really expected to be attacked by the Spanish. They were just a small town, one of many along the Maas River, not a great city like Haarlem or Alkmaar. Unfortunately for them, though, they stood in the way of the Prince of Parma. If Berkdorp remained in Dutch hands during the Prince's invasion, it could stop supplies from reaching him along the road. So the Prince was sending one of his armies to capture Berkdorp.

The town council didn't know any of this. All they knew was that a Spanish army was coming. They remembered the "Spanish Fury," when a rogue army of Spanish soldiers had devastated Antwerp, killing at least 8,000 people. Would Berkdorp be treated like the towns of Mechelen, Zutphen, and Naarden, which the Spanish had plundered even though they had surrendered? At Haarlem the Spanish had tied the Dutch soldiers back to back, then thrown them into the river Spaarne to drown. The town council agreed: it was better to fight and possibly survive than to surrender to the Spanish and certainly be pillaged.

The defenders were a very mixed lot. Some of them were members of a civic militia called the Brotherhood of St. Sebastian, made up of citizens of Berkdorp who trained in their spare time. There were almost 2,000 of these, but the militia had always been as much a social club as an army. The officers may have had their group portrait painted by a famous artist from Amsterdam, but that didn't make them good soldiers.

Like most Dutch communities, Berkdorp employed a company of 150 *waardgelders*, professional soldiers, to guard the town gates. They weren't as good as the real Dutch army, but they were much better fighters than the townspeople. Their captain, Maarten van Schooten, had been a drill instructor before the war, teaching soldiers how to use their weapons. Now he drilled the Brotherhood every day, trying to prepare them for when the Spaniards attacked.

Finally, there were a few hundred Beggars, a ragged mix of piratical patriots known as much for plundering as for fighting. The Beggars had done most of the fighting in the early years of the revolt, but they were loyal only to themselves, not to the town. The townspeople could never be sure if they were a blessing or a curse, and many feared them as much as the Spanish.

Luckily for Berkdorp, everyone was ready to do his or her part in the defense. Many of the women had heard of Kenau Simonsdochter Hasselaer. During the siege of Haarlem, she had poured vats of burning **pitch** on Spanish soldiers trying to climb the town walls. And so the women of Berkdorp had already started to prepare wreaths of straw that they would dip in pitch and throw at Spanish attackers.

Would all this be enough to stop a Spanish army full of experienced soldiers? While the town council worried and the women prepared to defend Berkdorp's walls, Captain van Schooten of the *waardgelders* was busy planning how to prevent the Spaniards ever reaching the town walls.

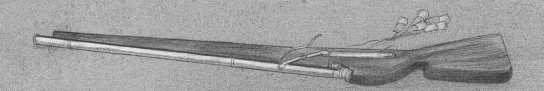

Brotherhood of
St. Sebastian

Waardgelder

Beggar

Townswoman

29

Attack and Sortie

For a month the Spanish trenches continued their advance day after day. For the Spanish, everything was routine – or as routine as work can be with cannonballs whistling overhead. Early one morning, that changed. The first sign was a terrible cannonade from the Dutch guns. Gabions were torn apart and wagons smashed, and the Spanish sappers huddled deeper in their trenches. After a few minutes the clash of swords and the thunder of muskets could be heard. The Dutch had launched a sortie!

The *waardgelders* swarmed out of the town, through hidden gates called *sally-ports*. They raced towards the besiegers' trenches. Workers and sappers fled in every direction, seeking to escape the ferocious Dutch troops. Now the Spanish camp was alive with activity, as captains urged their men forward to rescue the endangered sappers. Would they arrive in time?

The Spanish had not been totally unprepared. The trenches were studded with small **redoubts** every 200 meters (650 feet) or so, each holding a squad of infantrymen. These soldiers rushed out to do battle with the Dutch. While some of the Dutch soldiers held them off, others tried to destroy the Spanish trenches. Militiamen toppled gabions and set them alight, wrecked equipment, and smashed the sappers' tools. Reaching a few of the attackers' cannons, the Dutchmen drove a metal spike into the **touch-hole** of each, "spiking" the guns and damaging them beyond repair.

Suddenly the Dutch began to retreat. Captain van Schooten of the *waardgelders* had seen the approaching Spanish forces. His men had done enough damage for one day; they weren't ready to tangle with those veterans. The Spanish let them go, protecting what was left of their trenches. The

Dutch had done damage, but nothing that couldn't be repaired. They had delayed but not stopped the Spanish assault.

All was quiet for a few days as the Spanish repaired their trenches. But another surprise lay in wait for them. Outside the lines of circumvallation, a small Dutch force lurked. They had been sent from the main Dutch army to help Berkdorp, but they were far too weak to defeat the full Spanish army. So far they had limited themselves to harassing the convoys of wagons that brought supplies to the Spanish. But now they took a dangerous new step and began an attack on the Spanish lines.

Amid the violent cracks of muskets and arquebuses *(see page 33)*, the Spanish commander wondered – was this really an attempt to break the siege? He realized the truth too late: the Dutch attack was merely a diversion! On the other side of town, a hand-picked force of horsemen galloped up to the lines of circumvallation. The diversion had stripped the lines of Spanish troops, allowing the Dutch reinforcements to swiftly cross the lines and race for the town. Catching the Spanish flat-footed, they quickly reached safety. A gate opened and they triumphantly rode inside. Although the riders were too few to make a real difference in the defense, they brought with them a small but valuable cargo. Each man had tied a few bags of gunpowder to his saddle – enough ammunition to sustain Berkdorp for several weeks. Their leader was an experienced captain who had served under William the Silent, the leader of the Dutch revolt. He brought new hope to the town council. The Spanish could be defeated!

| January | February | March | April | May | June | July | August | September | October | November | December |

Reinforcements

Sortie

Trench

The Dutchmen drove a metal spike into the touch-hole of each cannon, damaging them.

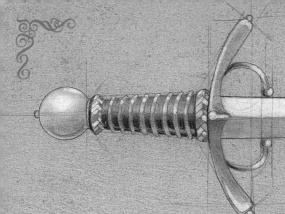

Tools of the Trade

The forges of the Spanish army were busy for days after the Dutch raid. Dented armor needed straightening and broken weapons needed fixing. The Spanish and Italian troops had brought their weapons from the armories of Lombardy in Italy, but anything that the army itself couldn't fix would be replaced from the great arsenals of Liège (in what is now Belgium). It was important to fix anything that might conceivably be reused, since there would not be enough replacement equipment coming from Liège. A pike and corselet – the body armor of a pikeman – cost 30 florins (the same as a year's supply of bread), and the Spanish were running short of money. If there was not enough equipment, no one wanted to be the man who had to do without.

Four of every ten Spanish infantrymen were armed with the pike, an excellent weapon for fending off enemy cavalry or skewering enemy infantrymen. Horses simply would not charge towards a forest of pikes. Because pikemen had to stand between attacking cavalry and the other Spanish soldiers, they wore the heaviest armor in the army – covering their torso, arms, and thighs.

Five out of ten men in the Spanish infantry were armed with the arquebus, the most common handgun in Spanish service. This primitive gun could fire a lead ball that weighed 43 grams (1.5 ounces) a distance of over 137 meters (150 yards), farther than the length of a football field. Protected by the pikemen, the arquebusiers generally wore less protection, making do with a stiff leather jacket and a steel helmet.

The last tenth of the Spanish infantry carried the musket, a new weapon invented by Spanish engineers. The musket was slightly larger and heavier than the arquebus, but otherwise similar. It shot farther than the arquebus and could penetrate body armor more easily, but it had to be fired from a forked rest. Like the arquebusiers, musketeers wore only a jacket and helmet for protection.

In all handguns, the gunpowder that propelled the lead ball was lit by a smaller quantity of powder in the priming pan. Both the arquebus and the musket used a matchlock mechanism, where a lit match ignited the powder in the priming pan. The matchlock was a very poor firing system because wind, rain, or an accident might put the match out. In fact, matchlocks failed to fire up to half the time.

A costlier, but more effective, way of igniting the powder was the wheel-lock. Invented in Germany, the wheel-lock used a striker wheel to create sparks that lit the powder. Although the wheel-lock was superior to the matchlock, the extra expense meant that it was mostly used on pistols carried by cavalrymen – who would find it difficult to handle a lighted match.

Handguns such as the musket or arquebus were far slower to fire than a good-quality bow such as the English longbow. It could take several minutes to reload the gun after a single shot, while an archer could fire a dozen arrows in the same time. However, the handgun had one major advantage: it was simple to use. While it took years of regular practice to train even an average archer, only a few months were enough to make any peasant an expert handgunner.

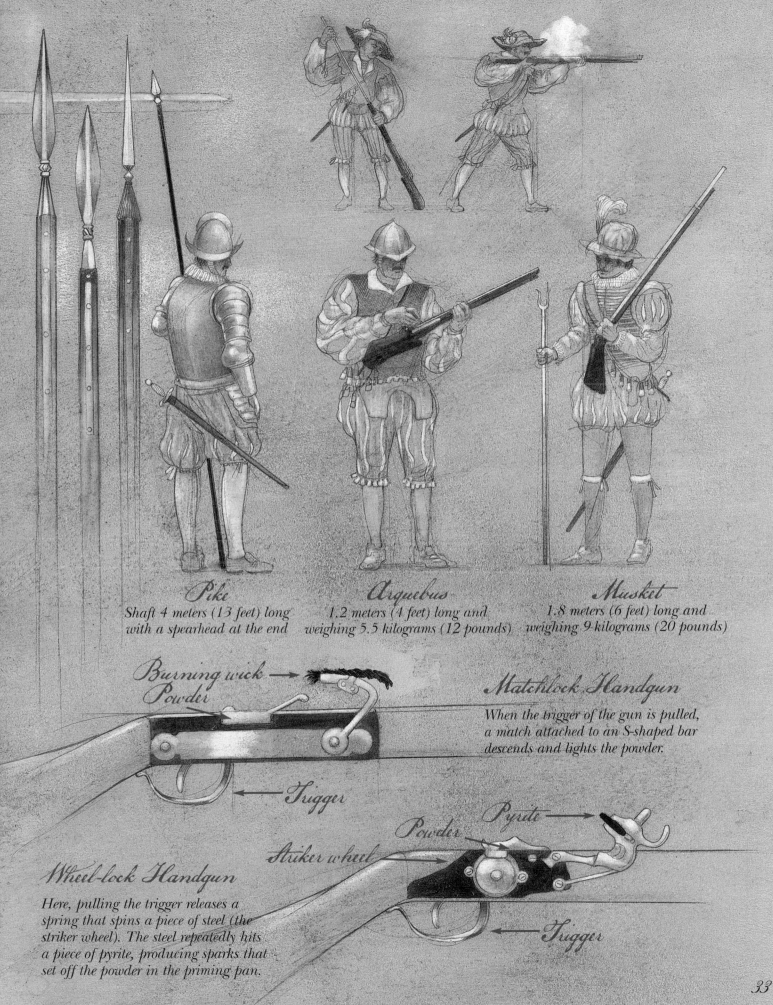

Pike
Shaft 4 meters (13 feet) long with a spearhead at the end

Arquebus
1.2 meters (4 feet) long and weighing 5.5 kilograms (12 pounds)

Musket
1.8 meters (6 feet) long and weighing 9 kilograms (20 pounds)

Burning wick →
Powder

Matchlock Handgun
When the trigger of the gun is pulled, a match attached to an S-shaped bar descends and lights the powder.

← Trigger

Powder
Pyrite →
Striker wheel →

Wheel-lock Handgun
Here, pulling the trigger releases a spring that spins a piece of steel (the striker wheel). The steel repeatedly hits a piece of pyrite, producing sparks that set off the powder in the priming pan.

← Trigger

The Grand Arsenal

A cannonball smashed into the town wall, sending piles of dirt down into the moat. The soldiers in the guardroom at the foot of the wall cautiously looked around, then returned to their game of dice. By now the roar of cannons was simply routine.

The Spanish had dragged more than 45 cannons into position to hammer the Dutch defenses. General de Guevara hoped they would batter a hole in Berkdorp's walls for his men to march through, or at least that they would destroy the Dutch cannons sitting on the wall.

The general had paid a high price for the guns: his artillery train had cost as much as the rest of his army combined. He had paid for hundreds of men and horses to move the guns and the enormous piles of cannonballs and gunpowder they were consuming – more than 1,000 cannonballs for each gun. His wall-smashing 24-pounders used a half ton of gunpowder for every 40 shots, and each shot cost as much as a soldier's monthly pay. The general had written to the Prince of Parma for more money, and he still worried that the cost of firing his cannons might bankrupt him. Still, it was better to spend gunpowder than lose men, since sickness was beginning to gnaw away at his army.

The most important cannons were the 24-pounders (also called *demi-cannons*), named for the weight of cannonball they threw (24 pounds/11 kilograms). Even heavier guns existed. The general had heard of a cannon owned by the Turkish sultan that threw an 800-pound (363 kilogram) shot – the weight of a full-grown cow. The 24-pounder was the lightest cannon that was capable of punching a hole through fortress walls.

Most of the army's 24-pounders were concentrated in the "grand battery," a collection of almost 30 guns. Each gun sat on a wooden platform that stopped it from sinking into the mud, and was protected in the front by earthworks reinforced with gabions and sacks of wool. Other, smaller cannons were used to shoot at the men on the town walls.

The Spanish guns were certainly making life difficult for the Dutch soldiers on the wall, but so far they were doing very little damage to the wall itself. The general wondered how many shots it would take to smash the hole he needed. Would the gunpowder supplies last for the entire siege? The general decided it was time to increase the pressure while he could still afford it – and sent for his chief gunner.

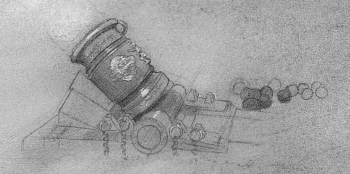

| January | February | March | April | May | June | July | August | September | October | November | December |

#1: The Gunpowder

Gunpowder is put down the barrel of the cannon, either loose or in a linen bag, followed by a wad of hay.

#2: The Cannonball

The cannonball is rammed down the barrel, then finer gunpowder is poured down the touch-hole.

#3: The Match

A lit match in the touch-hole ignites the fine gunpowder, setting off the main charge in the barrel and hurling the cannonball towards its target. The barrel is swabbed out with a wet mop before the next shot to extinguish any embers that might set off the next batch of gunpowder early.

#4: Fire!

Firing a cannon is a complicated task, but an experienced crew of gunners can fire 10 to 20 shots in an hour.

Bombarding the Town

The Spanish chief gunner was busy trying to smash a particularly pesky Dutch cannon. Like the rest of the Dutch guns, it had been firing at the diggers in the trenches, as well as at the guns of the grand battery. Now the Spanish were firing back, trying to destroy the Dutch gun.

While most of the men who worked the cannons were simple soldiers, a few – like him – were master gunners. Experts in the arts of gunnery, they knew the secrets of making gunpowder and the science of ballistics. Founded by the great Italian Niccolo Tartaglia, who had discovered that cannonballs in flight traveled in an arc, not a straight line, ballistics helped gunners use charts and diagrams to aim their cannons more accurately.

Unfortunately, the cannons of the time were so crudely made that they rarely matched the ideal gun of the charts, so most gunners preferred to rely on their experience. The best-known master gunners in the Spanish army were, like the engineers, Italians, although some Spaniards were well known too. Being a gunner was dangerous, even in peacetime, because cannons – especially experimental ones – still had a tendency to explode without warning.

Now General de Guevara came to his chief gunner with a decision: they would switch from firing at the town walls to bombarding the town itself. Destroying their homes might convince the defenders to surrender faster.

The premier weapon for bombardment was the *mortar*. A very short-barreled cannon, the mortar flung its shots up and over the town walls in a high arc. Unlike regular guns, which fired solid shot, the mortar fired *shells* – balls filled with gunpowder that exploded. The bombardments would also use *hot-shot*, cannonballs heated until they were red-hot so that they would start fires.

Turning the artillery on the town itself was an uncommon tactic. Attackers usually wanted to take a town intact, while a bombardment could wreck it. If fires burned out of control, there might not be much town left the next day. Still, the general felt he was running out of time. With so many soldiers living so close together, disease spread easily. Every day, more and more Spaniards were coming down with **dysentery**.

A thunderous roar announced the beginning of the bombardment. Houses collapsed and stables were set on fire. Glass windows throughout Berkdorp shattered. Bucket brigades quickly formed to put out the fires. Luckily, the vital grain supplies were not hit. Neither were the gunpowder and other military stores.

The town council met in emergency session. Most of the councilors were ready to continue the fight. What other choice did they have? A few were starting to mutter about surrender – especially those who had lost homes or workshops in the bombardment. Surely accepting a small Spanish garrison was better than being massacred if Berkdorp fell? The captain from the cavalry raiders spoke last. If they could only hold out a little longer, he urged, perhaps the Dutch army would march down from the north and drive off the Spanish besiegers. The Dutch all knew about the Spanish reputation for cruelty. Would the men of the "Spanish Fury" really be merciful now?

| January | February | March | April | May | June | July | August | September | October | November | December |

Ballistics

Dysentery: A painful and potentially deadly disease spread through contaminated food or water.

Under Siege

Despite the problems and dangers the siege brought, daily life continued in Berkdorp. Families still had to be clothed and fed, and not everyone was constantly at work on the defenses. In the streets, children played a game they called *goos en papen* (Sea Beggars and Catholics, like the modern Cops and Robbers). Artisans continued their work, and servants kept at their tasks – although both groups replaced local gossip with rumors about the enemy trenches.

Even as the town council resolved to continue the fight, they were faced with a new dilemma. Berkdorp had been well provided with food when the siege began, but the Spanish stranglehold had made it impossible to acquire new supplies. The population had swelled when the inhabitants of the town's suburbs came inside, and the food situation had become precarious. At first, the town council had collected excess food from the townspeople and countryside, reselling it to those who had no food. Now the council realized a more drastic approach was needed. Without strict controls, the food supply would never last. All grain had to be **requisitioned** by the town, then **rationed** back to the people in small amounts.

Before the siege, Berkdorp had enjoyed a wealth of market gardens, small plots where vegetables were grown for sale. Now most of those vegetables had been eaten, and the townspeople had learned to live on only cabbages and turnips – the easiest vegetables to store. All livestock (cows and pigs) had been requisitioned as well, and once they had been slaughtered, horse was the only available meat. Before the siege, no one would have dreamed of eating a horse, but now it was considered a delicacy. At least the wells meant there was no shortage of water.

With rations so small, every person's share counted. In houses where someone had died, the living sometimes tried to conceal the death so they could continue to draw the deceased's food ration. With all the shortages, morale began to fall. Some of the Beggars, unhappy with their food rations, started complaining. The council was worried that they might desert if they didn't get more food – but there was none to spare.

Requisitioned: Taken over
by a town or government
for its own use.

Rationed: Given out
in small amounts.

39

Life in Camp

As the siege dragged on, the Spanish soldiers made themselves as comfortable as possible. The army had been a city on the move before, but now it was a shantytown sprawling across the countryside. The 12,000 camp followers who had accompanied it from Italy had been joined by others from all across the Netherlands. Many were *sutlers*, selling food and goods and giving loans when pay was late. If the town was stormed, the sutlers would buy the heavier booty – everything that was too large or bulky for a soldier to carry – for a fraction of its value, then resell it elsewhere. Lots of the other camp followers were valets and servants, called *mozos* in Spanish. Each captain hired four or five to care for his tent and clothes, but a regular soldier would have to be rich to afford even one.

The most controversial of the camp followers were the prostitutes. Some commanders thought they were an immoral scourge and banned them. The Dutch punished known prostitutes with flogging. Others thought trying to ban them was hopeless. In the Spanish army a 1574 decree allowed five for every 200 men. Regardless of the official rules, every company attracted the attention of a few.

The last group of camp followers, wives and children, were also frowned upon by the army. Some commanders believed that women promoted mutinies. Despite this, many soldiers were married, often to the children of other soldiers (called "daughters of the garrison"). The wives and children followed the army even in the field. A wife helped support her family in a variety of ways: by sewing, spinning, midwifery, washing clothes, or peddling goods. When pay was late, her earnings could keep the family from starving. Every wife feared the onset of a battle that could mean the death of her husband. It was hard for a poor widow to stay alive, and many were forced to marry another soldier in order to survive.

The death rate was even higher in camp than on the battlefield. Bad hygiene made every camp a breeding ground for disease: typhus, smallpox, plague, typhoid, dysentery, and syphilis. More unusual was *el mal de corazon* (trouble of the heart), a sort of psychological trauma that more modern doctors would have called "shell shock" or "post-traumatic stress disorder." In total, many more men died from disease than in battle. Even soldiers who survived tended to be somewhat disfigured, with sores from smallpox or syphilis, scars from old wounds, and rotting teeth.

On the move, the army's food never came from one place for long. Now, it had to. To feed so many mouths in enemy territory, the cavalry scoured the countryside for anything they could find that hadn't been hidden by the peasants. The most orderly way of getting supplies was through a system of "contributions." Each village was told what it should provide to the army and warned that failure to comply would mean the burning of the village. For now, the army was still in good shape – with enough food for all – but everyone wondered if they would be able to outlast the Dutch.

The Outworks

From his tent, General de Guevara could see the whole siege spread out before him. His trenches stretched forward towards the intricate shapes of the Dutch defenses. His bombardment had clearly not convinced the Dutch to surrender. Attempting to starve them out would take too long – the money he had requested from Parma had not yet arrived. He had to press forward and storm the town. Unfortunately, the town wall was not the only line of defense. In every direction, **outworks** threatened any foolish attacker.

Outworks were sections of a fortress outside the main wall (also called the *enceinte*). They were designed to expand the area a fortress controlled, enclosing a suburb or important hill, or overlooking a key bridge. They also ensured that any attacker would suffer a withering crossfire if he tried to attack the enceinte without first eliminating the outworks.

One of the Dutch outworks – a *hornwork* – sat right next to the path of the Spanish trenches. It had been built to stop an attacker from placing his guns on a hill that overlooked Berkdorp. Now that same hill overlooked the Spanish trenches. If the attackers kept digging forward, the Dutch would be able to fire down into their trenches with ease. The hornwork was well defended, with its own moat and two half-bastions (its "horns") producing a deadly crossfire across its front, making it resemble a miniature version of the main walls.

Not all of Berkdorp's outworks were built around hills. One reached down towards the river. It was a *crownwork*, which meant it added a full bastion in the center of its face to the two half-bastions on the corners (which made it look like a crown). The crownwork mounted guns that the Dutch could use to hammer any enemy who rode across the bridge there.

More outworks sat just outside the main walls, within the moat that surrounded Berkdorp. The *ravelin* had been the first type of outwork added to the basic *trace italienne* in Italy. Shaped like a triangle, it sat in front of the main wall between the wall and the enemy. It mounted extra guns to sweep attackers in the moat, and blocked shots aimed at the main wall. The ravelins produced a crossfire in the moat just outside the walls, making it difficult to assault a wall without first capturing and destroying the ravelins.

The Spanish trenches began to extend towards the hornwork. Hand-picked men came forward with rafts to cross the moat and scaling ladders to climb the walls. The Spanish guns silenced the cannons of the hornwork, and then the Spanish attacked. Veteran Spanish soldiers clashed with the beleaguered defenders, and the Dutch line slowly began to buckle. A few more minutes of hard fighting and the defenders fled back into the town. The Spanish pursued them, but at the last minute the Dutch destroyed the bridge that connected the hornwork to the main walls. All the Spanish could do was hurl insults at the Dutch defenders across the moat. Still, now that the hornwork had fallen, Berkdorp's days were numbered.

Steep slope makes an assault here impossible.

Outworks: Parts of the defenses of a fort or town outside the main wall, such as hornworks, crownworks, or ravelins.

Marsh

Marsh

Maas River

Crownwork

Guns on crown-
work can shoot at
Spaniards who try
to cross the bridge.

Moat

The Spanish
planned to
breach the
Dutch walls
here.

Hornwork and main
walls catch Spanish
trenches in a crossfire.

Ravelins in the
ditch add extra
guns to the
defenses, making
an attack harder.

Hornwork

Trenches

Defenders
flee from the
hornwork to
the safety of
the town
over this
bridge, then
destroy it
to prevent
pursuit.

A trench splits
off from the
main trench
to attack the
hornwork.

The Grand Battery

The Spanish camp

43

Mutiny

The grumbling had been going on for weeks, starting quietly and gradually growing in strength. Some of the soldiers had not been paid for months, and now they were getting angry. While the officers were sitting in their comfortable quarters, the men were roughing it. They were also doing all the hard work. So some of the soldiers were considering a terrible act: mutiny. Their grumbling turned into planning, and their planning into action.

It wasn't really the general's fault. He had no more control over the money supply than the men did. Every week he had written to the Prince of Parma, warning him of what was coming if pay chests didn't arrive from Antwerp on time. Money was short, as always, and buying the equipment to fight the war made it hard to pay for the soldiers. After all, a single 24-pounder cost as much as a month's supply of food for 800 men.

The uprising began among the German arquebusiers, who were some of the worst paid of the troops even when the money arrived on time. Soon the entire army was refusing orders. Officers were invited to join, as equals, with the common soldiers. When the officers refused, they were expelled from the camp. Soon enough, the mutineers signaled for a **parley**. They had selected a leader and a council. The mutineers even had a secretary and an official seal for their proclamations.

The general had seen mutinies before, and the demands were no surprise. The mutineers asked for all the pay they were owed, as well as the pay of their dead comrades (for their widows), plus a full pardon and permission to leave the army and the Netherlands. Finally, there would be a general muster so the soldiers who stayed could choose what unit they wanted to serve in.

The general agreed to the demands; there was nothing else he could do. Unfortunately, it would take time for Parma to find enough money. In the meantime, General de Guevara used what little money he had to pay the mutineers a fee called the *sustento*. In exchange, the mutineers agreed not to ravage the countryside and to defend the siege works if attacked by the Dutch.

Finally, the chests of gold and silver arrived, surrounded by the armed horsemen who had guarded the convoy against brigands or Dutch troops. The paymasters brought out bags of gold coins and the mutineers cautiously accepted their pay. The leaders of the mutiny made sure the men paid their debts, and then the soldiers were free to go.

Relatively few soldiers ended up leaving the army. They knew that getting home might be more dangerous than staying with the army. Peasants often held grudges against soldiers for past mistreatment, and newly paid soldiers made tempting targets. A royal guarantee of safe passage didn't necessarily stop a peasant from robbing an ex-soldier – even in Spain. After all, a dead man couldn't complain to the king. Only the ringleaders would leave army service, and they left because the Spanish government demanded it – no general wanted the ringleaders of a successful mutiny hanging around. It had not been the first mutiny for many of these men, and it probably wouldn't be their last.

Parley: A discussion between opposing sides — such as two armies.

45

Mining

The trenches had reached the moat. Pushed to exhaustion, the sappers raised a ragged cheer. Their work was done. It was time for the soldiers to take charge. The Dutch knew that the moment of decision was nearing.

On the outside of the moat was an area called "the covered way." It was the first line of defense for the main walls.

The palisade of wooden spikes that was supposed to block an infantry assault was gone, smashed to pieces by cannons. The trenches finished only a few meters from the Dutch defenders in the covered way, but the Spanish would still have to brave a withering fire to take it. The men were ready for action, and they were sure that they, veterans of a hundred actions, could beat the part-time soldiers who filled the Dutch lines. They began by throwing hand grenades made of iron or thick glass, which stunned the defenders, then charged over the top to attack them with drawn swords. They swept over the Dutch. Captain van Schooten of the *waardgelders* was stabbed in the chest. He fell backwards and was carried into the town, badly wounded. The Dutch retreated from the covered way, fleeing to the safety of the main walls.

Once the fighting for the covered way was done, there was no time to lose. The Spanish threw earth into the waters of the moat, building up a **causeway** the troops could use to cross. Engineers lashed barrels and planks together to make rafts and bridges. Gunners dragged cannons forward to fire at the Dutch on the walls. General de Guevara had hoped that his guns would smash a hole in the defenders' wall, but he had been disappointed. Clumps of earth and bricks had been blown into the moat, but the wall was still mostly intact. He would have to send his miners forward to open a proper hole in the wall before the final assault.

In the Middle Ages, *siege mining* had meant digging a tunnel under an enemy wall, then burning the wood that supported the tunnel roof. When the tunnel collapsed, the wall on top came down as well. Mining in the 16th century was even more impressive. Packing the tunnel with barrels of gunpowder, the attackers aimed to blow wall and defenders sky-high. A mine the Dutch exploded at the siege of Steenwijk was so powerful, it had torn men apart as it threw them into the air. Thirty or forty barrels were said to do the trick.

At some sieges, "deep" mines were started far from the defenders' walls. The miners dug secretly underneath the ditch until they reached an enemy bastion. Their explosion came without warning – a terrible surprise. Defenders tried to sabotage deep mines by detecting them early. Jugs of water, rattles, or bells could all be used to detect vibrations from digging. When the defenders discovered a mine, they began to build a counter-mine that connected to the attacking tunnel. Either this vented the explosion harmlessly or it let the defenders charge into the original tunnel and slaughter the miners. Vicious hand-to-hand battles often raged underground.

In the Netherlands, the presence of lots of water under the surface made it difficult to build those deep mines. The Spanish miners, hired from the coal mines near Liège, had a simpler job here: dig directly into the Dutch earthen wall and blast it apart.

Causeway: A bridge made of earth used to cross water.

The Moment of Decision

A thunderous crash announced Spanish success. Their miners had blown a hole in the wall. Was it wide enough? Braving the enemy fire, General de Guevara came forward to inspect. With musket balls whistling around his ears, he declared that the breach would do. Both sides knew that the moment of decision was near.

First, there would be a battle to clear the breach. The Dutch would try to block the gap with debris, wooden beams, and metal spikes. Then they would put their men behind those barricades. Instead of iron cannonballs, the Dutch guns would be packed with musket balls, chains, nails, and other bits of metal. Although these wouldn't go as far as a single cannonball, the sheer number of these smaller shots would make them even more lethal to the attacking infantrymen. The results would be horrific.

The Spanish might suffer terrible casualties breaking into Berkdorp: as many as one in five of the attackers could die. After that, things would get easier for the attackers and worse for the defenders. European custom allowed the soldiers to **sack** the town for three days – one to plunder, one to organize their plunder, and then one to restore order. At the siege of Magdeburg in Germany, where the assault coincided with an accidental fire, 25,000 people died and much of the town was destroyed.

Even once order was restored, the ordeal would not be over for the Dutch. They were officially rebels, and therefore not protected by the laws and customs of war. At Haarlem, the Spanish had tied most of the garrison back to back in twos and threes, then flung them into the river to drown. Even the townspeople might be put to the sword. Everyone knew the stories of Spanish atrocities, even if not all of them were true. There were many reasons to surrender before the breach was stormed. After that, de Guevara would find it impossible to hold his troops back.

The Dutch knew they had to decide. If they surrendered before the assault, they might be given reasonable treatment. The town council assembled to make that decision. Would they ask for a **truce**, to negotiate their surrender? Maarten van Schooten had died of his wounds the night before, so they turned to the captain of the cavalry for advice. He made a fiery speech for resistance. Had other towns not fought off the Spanish fiends before? Was not God himself on their side? If they kept the faith, they would have a victory.

The council were not so sure. Still, they had no desire to end up under the Spanish yoke – nor were they certain that the soldiers in town would even let them surrender. So, the decision was made. Fight on!

January | February | March | April | May | June | July | August | September | October | November | December

Sack: To plunder and destroy
a town after it is captured.

Truce: A temporary peace between opponents.

49

The Assault

That night, the rains poured and poured. Thunder boomed and lightning streaked across the sky. In the Spanish camp, tents flooded and wagons sank into the mud. The next morning, the camp looked like a disaster area.

Could the attack go ahead? General de Guevara felt he had no choice. His supplies were running short, the weather showed no sign of improving, and each day more soldiers were coming down with dysentery. If he didn't attack today, he might not have enough soldiers to attack with tomorrow.

Marshaling his troops, the general led them towards the town. But the muddy ground meant it took twice as long to march from the camp to the walls. Cannons bogged down in the mud, and the men had to constantly stop to pull them out. By the time the exhausted Spanish troops reached the moat, they looked more like mud-monsters than soldiers.

There they were faced with more bad news. Most of the bridges their engineers had built across the moat had been half washed away by the storm. De Guevara had prepared rafts in case the bridges were destroyed, but the floodwaters churned like rapids, making any crossing chancy. One raft tipped over while crossing the moat, pouring the men on it into the water. Unable to swim to safety in their heavy armor, the men drowned.

When the other soldiers saw this calamity, they refused to get on the rafts, even for three days' pay and the prospect of plunder. A few men managed to scramble towards the breach over the damaged bridge, but they were driven back by the Dutch cannons and muskets. The rest of the Spanish soldiers fled. The assault had failed miserably.

As he watched his men run back to the camp, all the general could do was hope that the Dutch would not choose this moment to launch a **sally** from the fortress and attack the disorganized mob of soldiers. Luckily for him, however, the Dutch were too exhausted even to think of attacking. Their men were weak from hunger and disease, and they too had no desire to cross the raging waters of the moat.

The next day, de Guevara ordered the demoralized Spanish army to pack up its camp. He knew that after disease, starvation, mutiny, and finally this failure, his men had had enough. Soldiers and camp followers streamed south as the Dutch celebrated their victory with ringing church bells. Berkdorp had survived! And without the help of the main Dutch army, either.

Not everything was cause for celebration. The townspeople were still living on scraps of horsemeat and turnips, the suburbs were ruined, and large parts of Berkdorp had been seriously damaged during the bombardment. Many in the civic militia had been injured or killed. Men, women, and children had died from starvation or sickness. Everyone in the town had lost friends, family members, homes, or workshops. The cost of victory had been high.

Sally: A sudden attack by troops in a fortification against their besiegers.

The Peace

The next year, Berkdorp's *waardgelders*, under a new commander, marched off to join the main Dutch army in the field. The war with Spain would last another half century. Prince Maurice, son of the Dutch hero William the Silent, would turn the Dutch army into the most disciplined in the world and would help spark a military revolution that reached across Europe.

The England of Queen Elizabeth would send aid to the Dutch, angering King Philip so much that he sent the mighty Spanish Armada against that country. That scheme too would fail, like all of Philip's great plans. Eventually, Philip II would die without having reconquered the Dutch. The Prince of Parma had died six years before his king. Later, Philip II's grandson would recognize the independence of the Dutch. At the end of the revolt, the towns of the Netherlands became the Dutch Republic, the largest of the few states in Europe not ruled by a king.

The Dutch were a seafaring nation, and during the war they had fought the Spanish all over the world. After the war, they turned their ships to peaceful pursuits and became a trading empire. The Dutch Republic entered its "Golden Age."

And Berkdorp? The Spanish never besieged it again. It only took a few years to repair the damage, and soon a visitor would never know there had been a siege at all. The siege became a story for the townspeople to tell to their grandchildren. Then it gradually faded away. Eventually, the town tore down its walls so that it could grow. No one ever mentioned the siege; who was interested? Centuries went by. And one day a historian came along. He knew a little about the Dutch revolt, and he asked – was there ever a siege here?

Author's Afterword

The Siege tells the story of an event that never happened. While some people and places described by name, such as the Prince of Parma or the town of Antwerp, are real, the town of Berkdorp and the armies that fought over it are not. Still, the type of events described in this book occurred in many of the sieges of the Dutch revolt. Tactics pioneered by the Spanish and the Dutch spread across 16th-century Europe. At the siege of Antwerp in 1832, sappers still dug their zigzag trenches towards the bastions of the fortress, like they had done in 1585. But new weapons invented in the 19th century changed fortifications like those around Berkdorp from military master-pieces into curiosities. When Europe went to war in 1914, the bastioned fortress was replaced by complex trench systems, and an age of warfare ended. Some towns have preserved their old fortresses and walls, and these are often worth visiting.

Further Reading

I first described 16th-century siege warfare in *Battle Stations! Fortifications through the Ages* (Annick Press, 2005), which explores the history of fortifications from Ancient Egypt through the 20th century. For a good introduction to the world of the Renaissance, try Nancy Day's *Your Travel Guide to Renaissance Europe* (Runestone, 2001). *The Renaissance* by Alison Cole (Dorling Kindersley, 1994) has more on the art and artists of the age, including occasional fortress designers Leonardo da Vinci and Michelangelo (see page 22 in this book). *Outrageous Women of the Renaissance*, by Vicki León (John Wiley, 1999), tells the stories of 15 important women – including Kenau Hasselaer (see page 28 in this book). Finally, for advanced readers, Christopher Duffy's *Fire and Stone: The Science of Fortress Warfare, 1660–1860* (1975; Book Sales Inc., 2006) is the best introduction to the world of siege warfare.

Acknowledgments

I would like to thank Sheryl Shapiro for her insightful advice and constant support, John Mantha for his fabulous artwork, Barbara Pulling and Barbara Hehner for their excellent editing, and John Sweet for his keen eye and helpful corrections. I am also indebted to the many great historians whose work I relied on in writing this book. Any errors are, of course, my own. Finally, I must thank Anne Sealey for her patience and advice, both related to this book and otherwise.

—S.S.

Index